BRITAIN IN OLD ⬝⬝⬝⬝⬝⬝ ⬝S

DONCASTER

GEOFFREY HOWSE

*This huge water wheel was built over the River
Cheswold in 1703, three years after a typhoid
epidemic that was caused by the drinking of
river water. It operated pumps to help provide
a cleaner supply of water and remained in
operation until 1916.*

SUTTON PUBLISHING LIMITED

Sutton Publishing Limited
Phoenix Mill · Thrupp · Stroud
Gloucestershire · GL5 2BU

First published 1998

Copyright © Geoffrey Howse, 1998

British Library Cataloguing in Publication Data
A catalogue record for this book is available from the
British Library.

ISBN 0-7509-1420-3

Typeset in 10/12 Perpetua.
Typesetting and origination by
Sutton Publishing Limited.
Printed in Great Britain by
Ebenezer Baylis, Worcester.

St George's Hall, located on the banks of the River Cheswold, *c.* 1910.

CONTENTS

The Grand Theatre, Station Road, Doncaster was opened in 1899 and was designed by the noted theatre architect John Priestly Briggs FRIBA (1869–1944), in a delicate 1890s interpretation of a Regency theatre. It is almost impossible to appreciate the Baroque façade today, as modern development has hemmed the building in. It became a bingo hall in 1961, and in recent years has been threatened with re-development. However, a campaign to save the theatre for future generations was mounted and has met with a great deal of support from local people, and it seems likely that the theatre will survive.

INTRODUCTION

I have greatly enjoyed compiling this book about Doncaster and the surrounding towns and villages which fall within its conurbation. I have attempted to cover as many areas and subjects as possible, but the availability of previously unpublished material has for the most part proved elusive. Having spent many hours searching through boxes of old postcards, visiting shops and markets in towns and villages throughout the West Riding and further afield, over many months and placing advertisements throughout the district, in my quest to produce a volume which is substantially different to other books available about Doncaster, I was greatly relieved when a chance introduction to Barry Crabtree allowed me access to a considerable portion of the material I have selected to include in this book.

Doncaster has for centuries been an important centre in the North of England. The geographical position of what was later to become Doncaster was recognised as being of considerable importance when the Roman fort of Danum was built. A small fragment remains but there is nothing left of the Norman castle built on the site of the fort, as this was replaced by the medieval church of St George, built around 1200. This church was destroyed by fire in 1853. Sir Gilbert Scott designed a church in the same style, which opened for worship in 1858 and remains one of Doncaster's most prominent features. Doncaster can still boast a rich architectural history despite the fact that it has an extremely poor record for preserving historic or architecturally important buildings. Many ancient buildings were destroyed within the last hundred years or so and, although Doncaster boomed both architecturally and financially during the Georgian period and increased its wealth as an important railway centre during the mid-nineteenth century, the early years of the twentieth century saw many fine buildings consigned to rubble; several magnificent country mansions in the surrounding area have disappeared forever. Even one of Doncaster's two rivers did not escape being tampered with: the River Cheswold was culverted during the second and third decade of the twentieth century and its existence is largely unknown by the people of Doncaster. As late as the 1960s Doncaster's gems were still being consigned to the scrap heap. Fortunately the Doncaster Civic Trust helped to prevent even greater vandalism when it published a report in 1973 recommending the designation of conservation areas in the town centre. The Bennetthorpe, Christ Church, High Street, Market Place and South Parade areas have been designated Conservation Areas.

Books such as this help to show the importance of preserving our heritage. Much of what is illustrated in these pages has been lost forever. A number of photographs have been included for their historical interest, although these images may be unclear. As we approach the millennium I hope it will serve to highlight the potentially disastrous consequences of uninspired town planning and encourage others to fight to retain buildings and traditions for the benefit of future generations.

Anthony St Leger (1731/2–86), from a painting by Thomas Gainsborough (1727–88).

CHAPTER ONE

CENTRAL DONCASTER

The premises of Smithson's gunmakers, formerly
T. Horsley & Son, gun and rifle manufacturer, situated in
Scot Lane in the early 1900s.

Two views of St George Gate. The top photograph was taken during the last quarter of the nineteenth century. The bottom photograph shows a similar view between the two world wars. With the exception of the church, none of the buildings shown in these photographs remain as St George Gate, which was once a direct route between the town centre and the parish church, almost disappeared when the ring road was constructed in the early 1960s. The greater part of what was once a thriving shopping street has now been engulfed by the section of the ring road known as Church Way.

The junction of St George Gate with Baxter Gate, *c.* 1910.

Construction of the ring road, 1961.

One of the earliest recorded photographs of the tower of St George's Church, taken from what may be part of French Gate.

The Doncaster Mutual Co-operative & Industrial Society Ltd, Station Road premises, 1910. Established in 1868, by 1911 it was advertising a membership of 13,000, had a share capital valued at £126,000 and annual sales of over £314,000. It advertised both town and country branches: town branches were to be found in Spring Gardens, Broholme Lane, Hyde Park, Station Road, St Sepulchre Gate, Abbott Street, Hexthorpe, Balby, Wheatley and West Laithe Gate; the country branches were in Conisborough, South Kirby, Goldthorpe, Askern, Edlington, Woodlands, Tickhill, Hatfield, Bentley, Bentley Road, Thorne, Norton, Arksey, Carcroft and Highfields. In 1910 the society returned over £37,000 as dividend to members on their purchases.

Station Road, *c.* 1902. On the left is the Doncaster Mutual Co-operative Society; on the right is the Benefit Boot and Shoe Company and in the centre is the Glyn Commercial Hotel, named after the Revd Edward Carr Glyn, Vicar of St George's and a principal promoter of the temperance movement in Doncaster. The Grand Theatre can be seen at the end of the road. Station Road was opened on 31 August 1902 and was the terminus for several tram routes. With the exception of the Grand Theatre, Station Road has been completely engulfed by modern development.

The Stirling Monument at the junction of Station Road and French Gate, *c*. 1903. The entire site is now occupied by the French Gate Centre, formerly known as the Arndale Centre.

High Street from Hall Gate, *c.* 1875. On the left, just before the scaffolding, is Doncaster's celebrated Mansion House, one of only three in England, the others being in London and York. The Mansion House was designed in 1744 by James Paine and built at a cost of £4,523 4*s* 6*d*, for use as the Mayor's residence. James Paine (1716–89) was a fashionable architect who worked in the neo-Palladian style. He worked on several country mansions in the Doncaster area, including the wings of Cushworth Hall, Serlby Hall, Sandbeck Hall and Wadworth Hall. Work commenced in the summer of 1744 but was delayed owing to the rebellion in Scotland; the Mansion House was ready for occupation by 1750. It contains a splendid suite of rooms, including reception room, ballroom, banqueting room and saloons. No longer the Mayor's residence, the Mansion House is still used for civic functions and other council business. It is a Grade I listed building.

Silver Street looking towards Sunny Bar, *c.* 1915. On the right, before the Palace Theatre, are the St Leger Tavern and Palace Buffet. The buildings described in the photographs in the following two pages can be clearly seen, but from the opposite direction. The Palace Theatre, also known as the Palace of Varieties, was built by the architects Ward & Ball; it opened in 1911 in Silver Street and staged live shows until 1920, when it became for a short time a cine-variety house and then a fully fledged cinema, changing its name to the Essoldo in 1947. This large theatre could accommodate 1,740 patrons. It closed in 1962 and was demolished in 1970.

Silver Street, 1901. Note the archway on the left (above which is a panel with carved figures) and the narrow unmetalled road.

Silver Street from a similar viewpoint, 1950s. The archway still exists and the carved panel is hidden behind an advertising sign for the Central Garage. The Essoldo Cinema stands where once were houses and the width of the road and pavements has been substantially increased, which necessitated the removal of the Georgian buildings, seen on the right in the previous photograph. These buildings were demolished during the late Edwardian period.

Silver Street, c. 1895. Martin's ironmongery shop is on the left in High Street and the tobacconist's shop belonging to Daniel Potergill is on the right in Hall Gate. The tobacconists was demolished in 1912, the Prudential Building being built on the site. The St Leger Tavern can be seen on the right-hand side of Silver Street, and the four buildings shown beyond were demolished in about 1909, prior to the construction of the Palace Theatre.

A policeman on his beat crosses Hall Gate at the Silver Street junction, c. 1905. The abundance of advertising signs on Potergill's shop can be clearly seen on the Silver Street gable end.

French Gate and High Street, 1894. The narrow opening on the left is Baxter Gate. Oliver's coffee rooms and their shop were noted for royal pork pies and all kinds of cakes, gingerbread and parkin. The County Fire Office provided insurance and the ironmongers, J.C. Walker, were next door. Across Baxter Gate in High Street were other shops, including G. Parkinson, boot and shoe maker, Leo Walker, basket-maker and F. Lummand, who made fancy chairs and wicker perambulators. The pump on the right was used to fill buckets to water the horses, and the water cart seen in the photograph crossing the end of Baxter Gate ran daily up and down the street watering the dusty road. All these buildings were pulled down when Baxter Gate was widened, shortly after this photograph was taken. In 1895 a new building incorporating a clock tower was constructed at the corner of French Gate and Baxter Gate, commonly known as 'Clock Corner', to the designs of the architect J.G. Walker. The clock in the photograph was taken down and incorporated in a building in Sunny Bar.

The Plant Brewery in Sunny Bar, *c.* 1950. The clock shown in the previous photograph can be seen here. The premises are currently occupied by Jaynes of Doncaster, who specialise in bridal wear.

Sheep being driven through central Doncaster, late nineteenth century.

Advertisement from the Royal Agricultural Show catalogue. This prestigious event was held in Doncaster between 2 July and 6 July 1912.

Advertisement from the Royal Agricultural Show catalogue, 1912.

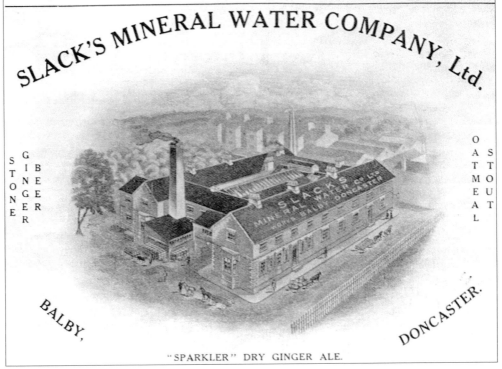
Advertisement from the Royal Agricultural Show catalogue, 1912.

PARKINSON'S

ESTABLISHED 1817.

The
Old
Butterscotch
Shop.

HIGH STREET,

DONCASTER.

Pastrycooks & Confectioners

ARTISTIC BRIDE CAKE MAKERS.

Sole Makers and Proprietors of the original

ROYAL   DONCASTER   BUTTERSCOTCH

AS SUPPLIED TO H.M. THE QUEEN AND ROYAL FAMILY.

PARKINSON'S CAFÉ

is renowned as the cosiest and
most convenient in the town.

Prompt Attention and Moderate Charges.

SOLE PROPRIETORS:

S. PARKINSON & SON (Doncaster), Ltd.

ESTABLISHED 1817.

Advertisement from the Royal Agricultural Show catalogue, 1912. This shows the celebrated Doncaster
business S. Parkinson & Son, and features a photograph of their well-known premises in High Street.

A Doncaster Corporation tram decorated for peace celebrations, November 1918.

The Hall Gate/High Street junction looking north, 1920s. The Reindeer Hotel can be seen on the left.

The Reindeer Hotel, which stood at the Hall Gate/High Street junction at the corner of Cleveland Street, is known to have existed on the site as early as 1782. The photograph dates from the early twentieth century. During a period of what can only be described as 'municipal madness', when many notable Doncaster buildings were torn down, the Reindeer Hotel was lost, much to the regret of many Doncaster citizens.

The Reindeer Hotel, 1920s or 1930s. Note the early traffic lights.

The corner of Cleveland Street at the High Street/Hall Gate junction, looking south, *c.* 1966. The Danum Hotel replaced the old Ram Hotel during the Edwardian period, and beyond is the ill-conceived, glass-fronted modern building which was constructed on the site of the Reindeer Hotel, and which is completely out of keeping with the surrounding buildings.

Homegoing racegoers in High Street and Hall Gate, St Leger week, 1903. The Ram Hotel was an old coaching inn. The premises of Mark Dowson, tailor and outfitter, can be seen on the corner of Cleveland Street. These premises, along with the Reindeer Hotel next door, were among the first buildings to be supplied with electricity in Doncaster in 1897.

The Mayor, Councillor J. Halmshaw, and the Corporation of Doncaster, 9 November 1909.

The laying of the foundation stone of the Girls' High School, 24 February 1910. The school was built on the site of Chequer House in Chequer Road. Alderman H.H. Birkinshaw declares the stone 'well and truly laid'. The school was officially opened on 3 October 1911.

Pupils and staff at the Doncaster British School, a forces school situated near the Racecourse roundabout, 1913.

Clock Corner, July 1912. Doncaster's streets were decked out with bunting and given a festive appearance when Doncaster was chosen to host the Royal Agricultural Show. Owing to an outbreak of foot and mouth disease several sections had to be deleted from the programme of events. The resulting attendance figures were considerably lower than the event held at Norwich the previous year, only 90,139 compared with 121,465.

In 1908 work commenced on the building of a bridge to span the Marsh Gate railway crossing. Known locally as the New Bridge, and officially as the North Bridge, it was designed by the engineer Edward Parry and constructed by the local firm H. Arnold and Son. The bridge was officially opened on 11 February 1910.

North Bridge, *c.* 1920.

North Bridge from a similar viewpoint to the photograph above, 1965. The Bridge Hotel and several buildings on the left were demolished in the early 1970s.

During the First World War a section of the southern side of St Sephulcre Gate was set back. The photograph shows no. 17, the business premises of W.D. Borrill, fish and game dealer, in the process of being demolished. Trading continued during this period of upheaval, as a temporary stall has been set up to the right in front of the Elephant Hotel, which has already been set back. The Elephant Hotel was demolished in about 1975.

Hodgson & Hepworth Ltd, St Sephulcre Gate, *c.* 1915. Established in 1872 as a grocery business, they eventually expanded their ranges, as can be seen from the signs beneath the windows.

The St Sepulchre Gate/James Street junction, *c.* 1910. Many of the buildings shown, including the YMCA were demolished during the 1960s when the Cleveland Street section of the inner relief road was constructed.

Shops occupying nos 31 and 33 and the Nags Head at 35 St Sepulchre Gate, from the junction with Station Road, 1920s.

St Sepulchre Gate near the Red House Corner, *c.* 1920.

Doncaster's oldest surviving business was established in 1781, when it occupied premises in French Gate. Business was later transferred to Baxter Gate before moving to St Sepulchre Gate in the 1850s. The Bell family remained owners until 1938 when the business was acquired by George Frampton, who retained the freehold and continued trading after his premises became part of the Arndale Centre in the 1960s.

The imposing premises of Hinchcliffe & Allott, drapers, at nos 13 and 14 High Street. Judging from the fashions on display, it seems likely that the photograph was taken during the Edwardian period.

Sandwiched between the Doncaster branch of the fashionable ladies' outfitters Mrs Melbourne, and the celebrated Doncaster firm of Samuel Parkinson, established in 1817 and famed for their royal butterscotch, was the Borough Printing Works, owned by Richard Henry Hepworth and situated at 49 High Street.

Military manoeuvres in High Street just before the Boer War, *c.* 1899.

St Sepulchre Gate from the junction with Station Road, *c.* 1920.

A late-Victorian view of the Primitive Methodist Connexion chapel, built in Cleveland Street and opened in 1854.

Cleveland Street, 1922.

Hall Gate and High Street in the early motoring age before the First World War. The cottages on the right were demolished in the 1930s and the Ritz cinema occupied the site from 1934.

A similar view, about twenty years later.

The Angel & Royal Hotel, which was situated next to Matthew Henry Stiles & Son's chemists in French Gate, *c.* 1900.

Boots the chemist, 1920s. They came to French Gate in 1907 when they took over a shop previously owned by Doncaster chemist Edwin White & Sons.

The Baxter Gate premises of Freeman, Hardy & Willis Ltd, who proudly boast that they are the largest boot and shoe dealers in England, 1920s.

Towards the end of the last decade of the nineteenth century John May established a clothing business at 110 St Sepulchre Gate at its junction with West Street. This photograph, taken before the First World War, shows his original shop. The premises were rebuilt in the 1930s and suffered bomb damage in 1942. The family continued to trade until 1988, when the business closed.

Baxter Gate looking towards the Market Place in the distance, *c.* 1912.

A procession to call men to arms took place in 1898. Here it passes along High Street, watched by the Cuttriss family from the balcony of their home above Archibald Ramsden's shop.

Hall Gate on St Leger day, 1903. Many prominent Doncaster residents lived in the High Street during the eighteenth century. By the last quarter of the eighteenth century the building of well-proportioned Georgian houses had expanded into Hall Gate. These houses were particularly attractive to the professional classes. Because of the large number of doctors' residences in Hall Gate, it later became known by locals as the Harley Street of Doncaster.

Horsefair and Waterdale, 1900. In the centre background is Trinity Presbyterian church.

The same view, 1968. The Presbyterian church became Camelot's public house and is currently known as The Edens.

The premises of Robert Farr & Sons in Baxter Gate, *c.* 1910.

Hopkinson Bros, 49/51 Cleveland Street, 1890s. They made and repaired washing and wringing machines, sewing machines and bicycles. Bernard Cuttriss later occupied these premises, first running a garage from them and later a model shop.

The Guildhall, *c.* 1890. It was built in French Gate on the site of the original Angel & Royal Hotel. Much to the regret of many Doncaster residents, it was demolished in the late 1960s.

Station Road from Church Way, mid-1960s.

The Doncaster offices of the West Riding County Council, formerly the Glyn Temperance Hotel, Station Road, 1971. The building which stood next to the Grand Theatre was demolished when the Arndale Centre was extended.

The Arndale Centre and Clock Corner, 1968.

The day Doncaster Corporation Tramways opened for business in Station Road, 2 June 1902.

Geese on their way to market through the streets of central Doncaster, early 1900s.

The Three Horse Shoes. This building was constructed in 1914 and replaced an earlier public house bearing the same name. It stands in Town End and is situated adjacent to the bridge known as St Mary's Bridge or Mill Bridge.

The *Doncaster Gazette* printing offices, taken from the corner of Printing Offices Street and Pells Close, c. 1920. The building was demolished in February 1980, having stood empty for thirteen years.

The vessel *Maud*, owned by Jack Gray of Levitt Hagg, lies with its back broken against Marsh Gate Bridge, early 1900s.

Marsh Gate Bridge, May 1932 – when there was extensive flooding throughout the Doncaster area. Water levels rose so high that the surrounding streets were under water.

The old prison in Factory Lane, *c.* 1880. The studded oak door had a large lion's head knocker, and a peep-hole at eye level.

Doncaster railway station, early 1900s. Surprisingly, Doncaster has only ever had one railway station, even though in 1853 the Great Northern Railway Company made the town the headquarters of their engine- and coach-building plant.

Hall Gate, 1903. Shepherd's, on the left, sold the latest fashions. The white-fronted cottages next to Stanley's tobacconists were demolished for the construction of the Ritz (later called the Odeon), which opened on 26 November 1934.

Hall Gate from a similar viewpoint, 1968.

A view of Hall Gate looking towards High Street, 1968.

Hall Gate from the point which was later to be known as Gaumont Corner, early 1930s.

South Parade from Hall Gate, *c.* 1928. The cinema on the left opened as the South Parade Cinema in December 1920. It was renamed the Majestic a few years later and was demolished in 1933. The cinema became part of the Gaumont circuit in the late 1920s. The new cinema built on the site was named the Gaumont Palace and as the years went on was known simply as the Gaumont.

The Gaumont, shortly after the building was refurbished in 1968. As well as operating as a cinema, the Gaumont also had full stage facilities. It had a large capacity, and during the 1960s many well-known pop groups, including the Beatles, performed there. Pantomimes and musicals were also a feature at the Gaumont. However, when the Gaumont was converted to a three-screen cinema, the building work facilitated the removal of the vast majority of seats in the stalls, which cut its capacity to just over 1,000, and reduced its attraction as a live performance venue to some extent. In 1984 I presented a musical there myself. As an impresario, I had *The Wind In The Willows* on a forty-seven-week tour. It received its world première performance at the Alhambra Theatre, Bradford, in September 1983. When the production played for a week in Doncaster the miners' strike was at its height, a teachers' strike prevented any school parties visiting the theatre and, to put the icing on the cake, a local transport strike took place during the week we appeared there. Needless to say, our appearance in Doncaster was not one of the most successful on record! In 1987 the Gaumont changed its name to the Odeon. Live performances are currently not a feature there, as the new Dome, in Doncaster Leisure Park in Bawtry Road, stages many of the major attractions visiting Doncaster.

Looking through the archway into Milners Yard in the Great North Road.

Doncaster railway station, 1898. On the forecourt are eight hansom cabs, five growlers, five landaus and twenty wagonettes. Meals were prepared for the cabbies in the hut on the right of the photograph.

Doncaster railway station, 1968. Several private cars are parked on the forecourt and three Ford Zodiac taxis wait for passengers.

Two views of Town Moor Avenue, *c.* 1910. Town Moor Avenue extends from Wheatley to Leger Way. The open views across Town Fields make residences in this avenue as highly desirable today as they were when these photographs were taken.

CHAPTER TWO

THE MARKET PLACE

The staff of John W. Brooke, saddler and harness maker,
pose for the photographer in the doorway of their Market
Place premises, c. 1900.

The Corn Exchange, *c.* 1900. Constructed on a site adjacent to the Market Hall in a Mixed Renaissance style to the designs of William Watkins, it has now been restored and presently serves as an indoor market.

An engraving of Doncaster Market Place, 1840s. It shows the ruins of the former parish church of St Mary Magdalene, which were exposed, much to the surprise of Doncaster residents, when the old seventeenth-century Town Hall was demolished in 1846. The ruins did not survive long and were torn down to allow construction of the Market Hall. Human remains have been uncovered from time to time when building or pipe-laying work has been carried out in the vicinity.

Two photographs taken moments apart, when the Theatre Royal (also known as the Royal Opera House) was being demolished, 1900. Note the absence of the young man standing in front of the portico in the bottom picture. The Theatre Royal was constructed in 1776, to provide a fitting place of entertainment for the distinguished visitors to the town during Doncaster Races. It was an elegant mid-Georgian theatre, constructed in the Palladian style. The Woolpack Hotel, which dates back to at least the first decade of the eighteenth century and is little altered today, can be seen on the right of both photographs.

The Market Place during the Boer War. The iron railings in the bottom right-hand corner belong to the Theatre Royal.

The busy Market Place, 1897. The corner of the Theatre Royal can be seen on the extreme right of the photograph. The loss of this architectural gem is just one of the many blackspots in Doncaster's destructive past.

The western side of the Market Place looking north, *c.* 1910. Market traders sell their goods on the site of the old Theatre Royal in the foreground.

Market traders take a break from setting up their stalls to pose for the photographer, 1910.

Properties in the south-west corner of the Market Place, *c.* 1914.

The Wellington Inn, which occupied the south-west corner of the Market Place. The Wellington Vaults, situated in Bowers Fold, serves as a reminder of this once popular town centre hostelry.

CHAPTER THREE

DONCASTER'S INDUSTRIES
& THE RIVER DON

Part of the screening plant at Maltby Colliery, c. 1912.

The sinking of Barnborough Colliery, 1912.

Barnborough Colliery (later known as Barnborough Main) Rescue Team, 1929.

The sinking of Upton Colliery began in 1924. This colliery had a relatively short life. Owing to a combination of geological faults and frequent occurrences of spontaneous combustion, production was often halted. By January 1966 only the washery was operating and the colliery closed. The photograph shows Upton Colliery in about 1929.

Hickleton Main Subscription Silver Prize Band, 1923. This photograph shows the bandsmen at Hickleton Main proudly displaying their trophies. Hickleton Main Colliery was situated in the village of Thurnscoe, some 9 miles west of Doncaster. For most of its life (1892–1988), it was one of the largest collieries in the country. During the 1930s there were 4,145 men working there and for many years the colliery produced over a million tons of coal each year. Ninety-six years of mining ended when the last coal was brought to the surface in 1988. It was kept open on a 'care and maintenance' basis, however, after being amalgamated with Goldthorpe Colliery. By 1994 all the shafts had been capped and the surface buildings demolished. Many collieries had a brass band.

Bentley Colliery, situated 4 miles from Doncaster near the village of Arksey, was sunk between 1905 and 1909 by Barber Walker and Co. A village named Bentley New Village was built between the old village of Bentley and the colliery to provide housing for the workforce. Coal production commenced in 1909. The photograph dates from 1912.

Bentley Colliery during severe flooding, May 1932. The colliery closed in 1993.

Work commenced on the sinking of two shafts for Brodsworth Colliery on 23 October 1905; it was situated near the village of Woodlands, 6 miles north of Doncaster. A third shaft was sunk in 1923. The photograph shows No. 2 headgear and behind it No. 1 headgear. Construction work continues – and it seems likely that the picture dates from 1907.

Surface workers pose for the photographer by No. 2 headstock at Brodsworth Colliery, c. 1910. The colliery closed in August 1989.

Bullcroft Main Colliery, situated near the village of Carcroft, was sunk in 1908. Coal was reached towards the end of 1911. Bullcroft New Village was constructed to provide homes for those working at the colliery.

Bullcroft New Village under construction, 1912. The colliery merged with Brodsworth Colliery in September 1970. All surface buildings were later demolished. The colliery village now forms part of Carcroft.

Denaby Main Colliery, just before the First World War. The sinking of two shafts for this colliery began in 1863. The colliery owners, Denaby Main Colliery Co. Ltd, started sinking another mine in nearby Cadeby in 1889, and the company name was changed to the Denaby & Cadeby Main Colliery Co. Ltd.

Doncaster Road in the village of Denaby Main, c. 1915. The houses in the village and the Denaby Main Hotel, shown here, were built and owned by the colliery. Coal production continued at Denaby Main until 1968, when the colliery was closed.

Cadeby Colliery, *c.* 1905. Sister pit of Denaby Main, it was sunk in 1889 and reached the Barnsley Seam of coal in 1893.

On 9 July 1912 there were two underground explosions at Cadeby Main Colliery. The first blast killed 35 men, and another 53 men died trying to reach those killed or injured in the first explosion. The disaster left 63 widows and 132 fatherless chilren. The photograph shows local people anxiously waiting for news of those involved in the disaster. Cadeby closed in 1987.

Striking miners at Cadeby Main Colliery, 1912. The strike was about minimum rates of pay.

In December 1911 the picturesque and fashionable spa town of Askern (see also p. 110) was changed dramatically when the sinking of Askern Main Colliery commenced. New house building increased the size of Askern considerably, and the onslaught of coal mining and an influx of newcomers, ended the halcyon days of the townspeople. However, the mine closed during the early 1990s, so perhaps Askern will once again be a fashionable place to visit after the millennium.

The winding engine in the No. 1 engine house at Askern Main Colliery, 1920s.

The temporary headgear is in place for sinking the shaft at Hatfield Main Colliery, situated near Stainforth, 10 miles east of Doncaster. Work commenced in January 1912.

Work was still continuing on the shafts at Hatfield Main Colliery as late as 1921. Here the completed concrete upcast shaft headstock is on the right, and the erection of a permanent steel headframe around the earlier wooden structure can be clearly seen.

A view of Hatfield Main Colliery after full production had commenced, 1920s. Following an announcement by British Coal of their intention to close the colliery in 1990, the management made a bid and bought it.

Thorne Colliery is situated in the village of Moorends on the eastern edge of the Doncaster conurbation. Despite the fact that preliminary boring commenced as early as 1902 and the shaft was sunk in 1909, Thorne Colliery was not completed until 1926. This particularly deep mine (921 yards) was sunk through heavy water-bearing strata, which caused many problems over the years. In 1956 the National Coal Board closed the colliery 'for two years' to enable essential repair work to be carried out to the shafts. It never reopened. However, during the following years new headgear was erected over the two shafts and during the 1980s British Coal carried out an exercise with the intention of reopening the colliery. It never happened. Thorne Colliery was taken over by RJB Mining Ltd and kept on a care and maintenance basis.

Colliery houses built for the workforce at Thorne Colliery, early 1920s.

The sinking of Edlington Colliery, 4 miles west of Doncaster, began in 1909, and in July 1911 the Barnsley Seam of coal was reached at what was a record depth at that time of 905 yards. The name was changed to Yorkshire Main Colliery. Following the miners' strike in 1985 an announcement was made by British Coal that the colliery was to close. Closure took place shortly after the return to work.

A view of Waterside Glassworks in Mexborough, c. 1920. In the foreground is the River Don. Mexborough railway station can be seen between the river and the glassworks, and the canal bridge is just beyond the station.

A repair shop at the Great Northern Railway headquarters, Doncaster, 1912. GNR established the headquarters of their engine- and coach-building plant here in 1853. Over 6,000 hands were employed in building locomotives and carriages at that time. The site covered an area of 80 acres, with an additional 55 acres of sidings.

GNR works, 1912: the machine bay in an engine repair shop.

GNR works, 1912: the wheel shop.

The lime quarries and kilns at Levitt Hagg, *c.* 1885. The riverside village of Levitt Hagg had a population of around a hundred at the time this photograph was taken. The poor state of the housing compounded by regular flooding, which caused contamination of the water supply, led to the village being abandoned and almost completely demolished in the 1950s. Only a few buildings remain in the area.

This view of Burcroft Mill at Conisborough shows piles of Baltic timber, brought from Hull docks by barge, in the foreground. The mill bored cannon during the early eighteenth century, but by the time this photograph was taken it produced sickles and turned the imported timber to make handles.

The River Don and its tributaries and canals played an important role in the development of Doncaster's industries. This view of the water-powered flour mill at Sprotborough shows the mill in the 1890s.

This photograph, taken after the canal was widened in 1908, shows that the water level has risen. The bridge was replaced in 1933 and the mill closed for business that same year.

Barges on the River Don deliver seeds to a crushing mill at the port of Thorne Waterside, *c.* 1910.

A laden keel spills wind from its sails to enable it to pass through the narrow channel of the canal swing bridge at Bramwith, *c.* 1910.

A horse-drawn keel makes ready to enter Sprotborough lock at the river/canal junction on its way to deliver grain from Hull Docks to mills at Mexborough and beyond.

A Hull-bound keel lowers its sail to pass beneath the bridge at Sprotborough, 1920s.

This vessel is at the river and canal junction at Conisborough. The keep of Conisborough Castle can be seen on the skyline on the left.

A laden keel heads inland up Sprotborough cut.

CHAPTER FOUR

THE RACECOURSE

Grandstand Road, 1920.

Horse racing has been a feature in Doncaster for over 400 years. Records refer to racing there as early as 1595, when William Sheardown in a pamphlet entitled *Historical Notices of Doncaster Races* mentioned a plan showing 'a former race course and the present one'. Racing continued in one form or another until it reached greater prominence around the beginning of the eighteenth century and was supported by the Corporation. However, records of events are scanty up until 1728, since which year more extensive evidence exists of the 'sport of kings' being practised in Doncaster. Early meetings were not considered to be anything other than local events. Then in 1766 the Doncaster Gold Cup was instituted and this raised the status of racing in Doncaster significantly. It is, though, the St Leger that has made Doncaster Racecourse one of the most famous in the world – even though the race played second fiddle to the Gold Cup for its first few years. The photograph shows the Race Committee in September 1895. Doncaster Race Week, during which both the Doncaster Gold Cup and the St Leger are held, takes place in September.

When what is now known worldwide as the oldest classic turf race was first run, it was simply entitled 'A Sweepstakes of 25 Guineas'. The St Leger Sweepstakes, to give the race its proper name (or Sellinger Sweepstakes if one uses the correct pronunciation of the family name, as has been the practice in Doncaster for generations), was not actually given a name until its third year. It was first run on 24 September 1776 as a sweepstake of two miles on Cantley Common, Doncaster (colts to carry 8 stone, fillies 7 stone 12 pounds), and was won from a field of five horses by 'Allabaculia', a brown filly owned by the Marquess of Rockingham and ridden by John Singleton the younger (nephew of the celebrated jockey John Singleton, who is sometimes referred to as 'the first professional jockey' and was painted riding 'Bay Malton' in the famous painting by George Stubbs). The horse was not named on the race cards, although it is shown in later records. At that time identification by colour, sex, pedigree and ownership were of greater importance. The second horse past the post in this first race was owned by a military gentleman by the name of Lt-Col. St Leger of Park Hill. The photograph shows 'Bayardo', winner of the 1909 St Leger, ridden by D. Maher and owned by Mr Fairie.

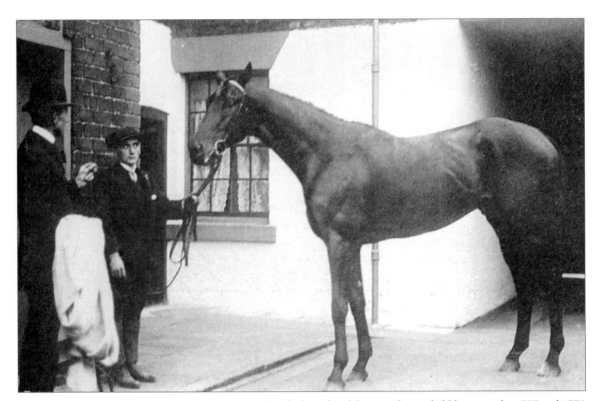

The St Leger was named at what has been variously described as a breakfast or a dinner, held between the 1777 and 1778 race meetings. However, there is considerable controversy as to where this meeting actually took place; some accounts say it was held at the Red Lion, Market Place, Doncaster (where two plaques, one attached to the outside of the inn and one inside, commemorate the event); others mention the Salutation in South Parade; and other venues mentioned include Warmsworth Hall and Wentworth Woodhouse, near Rotherham, seat of the Marquess of Rockingham. It cannot be said for certain where the meeting took place, but what is known for sure is that among the interested parties present (including the Stewards and members of the Corporation) were the Marquess of Rockingham and Lt-Col. St Leger. When it was proposed that the race should be named the Rockingham Stakes, Lord Rockingham, one of the greatest patrons of the turf in the eighteenth century and a powerful figure of racing in Doncaster, replied: 'No it was my friend St Leger who suggested the thing to me – call it after him.' But for Lord Rockingham's gesture, this great race could have been named after himself. Instead the Marquess goes down in history as being responsible for commissioning that greatest of all animal painters, George Stubbs, to paint some of his finest works, and also as a greatly loved Whig, having twice held the office of Prime Minister, dying in harness in 1782. Following that historic meeting, the first 'official' St Leger, run on the new course at Town Moor, was won by Hollandaise, ridden by George Herring and owned by Sir Thomas Gascoigne, one of the guests present when the race was named. The photograph shows 'Swynford', winner of the 1910 St Leger, ridden by F. Wootton and owned by Lord Derby. The racecourse has remained in the Town Moor to the present day.

Anthony St Leger was born into an Anglo-Irish family descended from a knight who crossed the English Channel with William the Conqueror. The name is derived from a seventh-century saint, Leger (sometimes known as Leodegarius), c. 616–79, who was the martyred Bishop of Autun. Born in 1731/2 at Grangemellan in Ireland, fourth son of Sir John St Leger, Anthony St Leger completed his education at Eton and Peterhouse College, Cambridge, and enlisted in the army, being gazetted subaltern at the age of twenty-two. In 1761 he married Margaret Wombwell, from Yorkshire, and was appointed Lieutenant-Colonel of the 124th Regiment of Foot. The regiment disbanded the following year and St Leger adopted a country lifestyle, settling at Park Hill estate near Firbeck, 9 miles from Doncaster – after which another race in the Doncaster calendar is named. Between 1768 and 1774 he sat in the Commons as MP for Grimsby and rejoined the army in 1779 as Colonel of the 86th Regiment of Foot. He was later appointed Brigadier General and saw active service on the West Indian island of St Lucia, where he served for a time as Governor. St Leger ended his military career with a staff post in Ireland with the rank of Major General. He died on 19th April 1786 and was buried in St Ann's Church, Dublin. His epitaph reads: 'In every station of life he merited the highest approbation.' This photograph shows the King's Entrance to the Grandstand, c. 1910. It was named in honour of Edward VII who was a keen racegoer, and when he was Prince of Wales, his horses twice won the St Leger – first 'Persimmon' in 1896, then 'Diamond Jubilee' in 1900 .

Some accounts mistakenly credit General St Leger's nephew as being the institutor of the race which bears his name, an honour which he was not eager to dispel. 'Handsome Jack St Leger', President of the Hell Fire Club, leader of the 'Dublin Bucks' and Groom of the Bedchamber of His Royal Highness the Prince of Wales, inherited Park Hill on the death of his uncle in 1786. He also patronised racing up until his own death in 1795, the landed estate he inherited from his uncle having been sold during his lifetime to the Wombwell family to settle gambling debts. Other accounts regarding the origin of the St Leger (including the entry in an encyclopedia which is possibly the most widely read in the English language), erroneously credit one Barry St Leger, a British soldier involved in the American War of Independence, as being the man behind the race. The photograph shows the St Leger Parade in September 1959. The race was won by 'Cantelo', ridden by E. Hide and owned by William Hill.

Princess Mary at Doncaster Races, September 1922.

The enclosure at Doncaster Racecourse, early twentieth century.

At the entrance to the racecourse, in the position now occupied by the junction of Carr House Road and the Great North Road at Racecourse Corner, there was formerly a pond known as Common Pond or Horseshoe Pond, on account of its shape. The purpose of the pond was to enable the wooden-wheeled wagons and carriages passing along the Great North Road to drive through the water, causing the wheel rims and spokes to swell, which prevented squeaking and wear. The pond was swept away during road improvements in the 1920s. This photograph was probably taken in the 1890s.

A later view of the Horseshoe Pond shows Tram No. 5, which came into service in 1902.

Looking from Horseshoe Pond down Leger Way, *c*. 1905.

His Majesty King Edward VII at Doncaster station after attending his last St Leger meeting, September 1909.

Excursion trains in the sidings at Doncaster station on St Leger day, September 1911.

A view of the grandstands at Doncaster Racecourse, 1912.

CHAPTER FIVE

TRANSPORT, AVIATION & THE MOTORING AGE

The forecourt of Doncaster station has been cleared of carriages and hansom cabs to enable the photographer to get a good view. Station officials stand in regimented fashion adding scale to the picture, which was taken in about 1900.

His Majesty King George V on a visit to the Royal Agricultural Show, Doncaster, July 1912. The king, having disembarked from the Royal Train, is welcomed at Doncaster station by the Mayor.

Doncaster manufactured one motor car, the Cheswold, which was named after a river flowing through the town. More than a hundred Cheswold cars were manufactured in the Doncaster works of E.W. Jackson & Son Ltd between 1910 and 1914. The engine was a 4-cylinder 15.9 h.p. with a four-speed 'crash' gearbox. Production ceased at the beginning of the First World War, and the marque was never revived.

J.G. Steadman established his firm in Silver Street in 1875. Originally horsebreakers, the business became involved with taxis, as well as providing vehicles for weddings and funerals. They also styled themselves as funeral directors. An early Steadman's taxi is seen here in service at the racecourse.

A Dennis motor bus owned by Steadman's, 1908. Steadman's became part of Hodgson Holdings in 1987.

In the early years of motoring W.E. Clark and Co. put on this display of motor vehicles outside their shop in Station Road. Extensive damage was caused to these premises in 1942 when a bomb was dropped in the Station Road/Trafford Street area during the Second World War, and two people were killed.

A pre-First World War display of motor cars outside the Woolpack Hotel in the Market Place.

Members of the Doncaster Motor Club line up in readiness for a trip to Newark, early 1900s. The vehicle in the foreground is a Morgan.

A meeting of the members of the Doncaster Motor Cycle Club at the Reindeer Hotel in Hall Gate, early 1920s.

England's first aviation meeting was held at Doncaster from 15 to 23 October 1909. Here Col. Samuel Cody, the American-born aviator who was killed in 1913 in a flying accident, can be seen flying his biplane.

Councillor T.H. Johnson, Mayor of Doncaster 1935–6, accepts the first bag of continental mail from Alderman A. Thomson in 1935. The aircraft belonged to Royal Dutch Airlines (KLM), regular visitors to Doncaster Airport.

CHAPTER SIX

AROUND DONCASTER

The post office, High Street, Carcroft, c. 1930. As well as providing the usual services one normally associates with a post office, tobacco was also sold and, more unusually, accumulators could be charged and petrol purchased there.

Barnborough, *c.* 1910. Note the recent repair to the roof of the cottage in the right foreground. Tiles have been used instead of the original stone slabs, seen on the lower portion of the roof. The use of 1 in stone slabs as roofing material was common throughout South Yorkshire, particularly during the seventeenth and eighteenth centuries, when stone quarried locally was readily available.

Doncaster Road, Conisborough, *c.* 1910. Historic Conisborough, with its magnificent eleventh-century Norman castle that featured in Sir Walter Scott's *Ivanhoe*, also boasts South Yorkshire's oldest surviving building, St Peter's Church, constructed AD 650–700.

Norton, *c.* 1900. At this time the main occupations for local residents were farming, mining and quarrying. Note how the older buildings have their gable ends facing the street, whereas the more recent infill buildings have been built front on. This is a feature throughout the village, which is just over a mile long and shaped like a foot.

Sprotborough station opened in 1894 on a spur line of the Hull & Barnsley Railway, constructed to transport coal to Hull. From 1903 until its closure in August 1964, the station handled freight only.

Main Street Sprotborough, looking west, *c*. 1910. A view of estate cottages that were owned by the Copley family. The Copley estate and Sprotborough Hall remained in the hands of the Copley family from 1516 to 1925. The estate was sold in 1925 and a year later Sprotborough Hall was demolished.

Main Street, Sprotborough, *c*. 1930. The eye is immediately drawn to the tower of St Mary's Church on the right: this is essentially an Early English and Perpendicular church with a Decorated tower. It has a thirteenth-century sedilia and piscina with a credence shelf. There is some particularly fine woodwork, which includes a fifteenth-century rood screen. A stone seat in the chancel, thought to date from the fourteenth century, is generally believed to be a frith-stool, the 'seat of peace' placed near the altar in some churches, being the last refuge of those claiming sanctuary within them.

The Don Bridge at Sprotborough, *c*. 1920. The ferry crossing at this point was replaced by a wood and iron bridge in the mid-nineteenth century. When West Riding County Council took responsibility for it, they demolished it and replaced it in 1897 with this girder bridge. Sprotborough is justly famed for its attractive waterside setting.

Sprotborough Weir, early 1920s. A flint mill stood to the left of the weir but was demolished towards the end of the nineteenth century.

The elegantly proportioned main building at Bawtry station served by the Great Northern Railway, *c*. 1915.

The neatly kept platforms at Bawtry station.

A meeting of the Fitzwilliam (Grove) Hounds, founded by Earl Fitzwilliam of Wentworth Woodhouse in 1858, at Bawtry Market Place, 15 March 1909. Major G.H. Peake of Bawtry Hall, with moustache and silk top hat, is mounted on his horse to the right of the picture.

Roche Abbey stables, 1912.

Askern is situated 7 miles north of Doncaster on the main A19 road. The medicinal properties of the mineral waters to be found there were first recognised in the eighteenth century. Six bath houses and the Hydro Hotel were built. The hotel (later to be known as the Old Hydro) was built in 1808 by Tom Humphrey. It stood in 3 acres of grounds and contained rooms for dancing, billiards, reading and writing, and was equipped with several types of baths including sitz, douche and sulphur. With the discovery of coal and the introduction of heavy industry in the town in 1911, its popularity as a spa declined. The Old Hydro was demolished in 1930. The Spa Hydropathic Establishment (the New Hydro), shown here, was built next to the Old Hydro in the early 1800s. It boasted thirty-two bedrooms, a billiard room and ballroom. After the decline of Askern as a spa it was taken over as a Miners' Welfare Institute in 1924 and, owing to severe mining subsidence, was demolished in 1960.

The Manor Sulphur Baths, Askern Spa. Known locally as the Manor Baths, they comprised a central bath area and promenade rooms in the wings. The boathouse can be seen next to the Manor Baths: boating was a popular pastime on Askern Lake. The boats shown here could hold up to twenty people.

Askern station, c. 1907. The station closed to passengers in March 1947 but continued to be used for goods traffic until October 1964.

Flooding in High Street, Askern, when the River Don burst its banks, May 1932. The two houses in the middle,right were once the Charity Baths.

High Street, Askern, during the Second World War. The '209' on the gable end of Victoria Terrace is a marker indicating where concrete blocks should be placed across the road in the event of a German invasion.

Hexthorpe Flats were acquired as a recreational area for the people of Doncaster by Doncaster Corporation, when they purchased the site and its abandoned quarries in 1902. Boating became a popular pastime and Henry Otley established a boathouse here in 1904, from which boats could be hired.

Hexthorpe Flats, *c.* 1905.

Spanskye Street, Hexthorpe, 1901. Workmen are laying a single track tramway, with a loop to allow trams to pass. A service ran into the heart of Doncaster until trolleybuses took over the service from 1930; they were subsequently replaced by motor buses. Doncaster's last trolleybus ran on the Beckett Road route on 14 December 1963.

Rainbow Bridge, which spanned the River Don at Conisborough. When the South Yorkshire Railway opened a line between Swinton and Doncaster in 1849 they built this bridge, seen here in 1924. In 1928 the bridge was demolished and replaced by one which could bear heavier loads.

Dearne Valley Railway constructed this viaduct across the River Don near Conisborough. Work was completed in 1907. The last train crossed it in 1951.

A view of South Parade, Bennetthorpe, looking towards the Doncaster war memorial. The memorial was designed by J. and J.H. Pearson of Manchester and unveiled on 12 March 1923. It features a figure of 'Grief' mounted on a plain obelisk.

Great Central station, Mexborough, *c.* 1905.

A view of Mexborough station from the opposite direction, *c.* 1905. Mexborough lies on the northern bank of the River Don, 6 miles west of Doncaster. In 1811 it had a population of 403. Potteries, ironworks, glassworks and coal mining increased the size of the town, which spread along the river bank northwards. By 1877 Mexborough had its own newspaper, the *South Yorkshire Times*, which is still widely read throughout the area.

Mexborough Ferry, *c.* 1900. The ferry boat at Mexborough allowed quick access from Mexborough to Old Denaby across the River Don; a long walk to the nearest bridge was the other option. The ferry operated until 10.00 p.m. A bridge was eventually built, but not until the 1960s.

The Druids Arms, Bentley, *c.* 1910.

A view of Levitt Hagg from Sprotborough, *c.* 1910. The barn in the foreground is now part of the Boat Inn.

The Swiss chalet-style main building at Norton station, *c.* 1905.

Stainforth and Hatfield station, *c.* 1930. Hatfield Main Colliery can be seen on the left.

The capstan-operated swing bridge at East Cowick. This original wooden Rawcliffe Bridge was replaced by a steel structure in 1925, and that was replaced in the 1960s by a fixed bridge constructed from concrete blocks.

The wooden canal swing bridge at Barnby Dun, *c.* 1920. A canal cut, fed by the River Don, left the river at Long Sandall. Several swing bridges carrying minor roads and farm tracks were required. One such is shown here.

Barnby Dun station, 1905. The line was widened in 1913 and the station was completely rebuilt. It closed in September 1967.

Flooding in Arksey after the River Don burst its banks, May 1932.

A meeting of the Fitzwilliam (Grove) Hounds in Rossington, 11 November 1909.

The attractive and historic town of Tickhill can trace its origins to pre-Roman times. It developed into a settlement of considerable size shortly after 1066, when William I rewarded one of his Norman supporters with the gift of several manors in the north of England, one of which included the lands around the area that later became known as Tickhill. There are many reminders of Tickhill's rich historical past, including the Friary which was founded in about 1260, and which is now a private residence, St Leonard's Hospital, founded in about 1225, Tickhill Castle gatehouse, the remains of the castle itself, St Mary the Virgin's Church and the Butter Cross featured in this early nineteenth-century photograph. It was built in 1777 and positioned at the convergence of major routes.

Tickhill station under construction, 1907. It opened for commercial transportation of minerals in January 1909 and for passenger traffic in December 1910.

Building work at Tickhill station nearing completion, 1909.

The Millstone Inn, Tickhill, before the First World War. This popular public house was situated within hearing of the bells of St Mary's Church. This church was sited on the edge of the original Anglo-Norman borough of Tickhill and was founded in the thirteenth century. Henry I granted the right to present vicars to Tickhill and to have the great tithes of the parish to the Prior of Nostel between 1121 and 1127. Much rebuilding work took place in the fourteenth century in the Perpendicular style, creating one of the finest examples of the style in the West Riding. Richard I licensed tournaments at Tickhill and, during his absence on the Crusades, his brother John seized the castle in 1191. When John became king in 1199 he spent over £300 on the castle defences. During 1321 and 1322 the Earl of Lancaster tried to call a Parliament at Doncaster. Civil war followed and in February 1322 Tickhill was besieged for three weeks. In 1540 John Leland, the traveller, described Tickhill as 'very bare' but its church was 'fair and large'. It is said that Oliver Cromwell remarked during the storming of Tickhill Castle in 1644, 'Tickhill, God help them', before the Royalist stronghold fell under Roundhead control. The castle was dismantled in 1648.

Tickhill enjoyed long prosperity as a borough, sending two members to the Parliament called by Edward I in 1295. However, the Middle Ages saw economic depression and a decline in the importance of the institutions on which Tickhill's prosperity depended. At some point between the sixteenth century and the start of the Industrial Revolution, following a gradual decline, Tickhill lost its status as a borough. The town's fortunes did not improve greatly during the eighteenth and nineteenth centuries. However, the 1851 census indicates some gradual improvement in the town's fortunes, with numerous rural crafts and trades being practised. Tickhill is now a small country town in a traditionally agricultural area. The last quarter of the twentieth century has seen considerable development, which has provided new homes for commuters. Its relative isolation remains one of Tickhill's principal attractions.

Acknowledgements

I am most grateful for the assistance I have been given during the compilation of this book. I would like to thank my personal assistant Mr John D. Murray, Mr Clifford and Mrs Margaret Willoughby, Mr Herbert and Mrs Doreen Howse, Mr David and Mrs Christine Walker, of Walkers Newsagents, Hoyland, The Hon. Lady Hastings, Harry Grounds of Class Method Ltd, Miss Tracy Deller, Ricki S. Deller, Miss Joanna C. Murray Deller, Miss S. Owen, Mr Dylan, Mrs Julie Wiggett, Mr A. Rombo, Miss Suki B. Walker, Mr Paul T. Langley Welch, Mr Simon Fletcher, Miss Annabel Fearnley, Miss Alison Flowers, Ms Mary Warren (proofreader), the many photographers whose work is featured in this book, including, Edgar Leonard Scrivens, Roy Colville and Luke Bagshaw; and finally I would particularly like to thank Mr Barry Crabtree for allowing me access to his extensive collection of old photographs.

BRITAIN IN OLD PHOTOGRAPHS

SUTTON'S PHOTOGRAPHIC HISTORY OF TRANSPORT

To order any of these titles please telephone our distributor, Littlehampton Book Services on 01903 828800
For a catalogue of these and our other titles please ring Emma Leitch on 01453 731114